# OHIO 4-H BLUE RIBBON COOKBOOK

**4-H Pledge:**

I pledge:
   My HEAD to clearer thinking,
   My HEART to greater loyalty,
   My HANDS to larger service, and
   My HEALTH to better living,
for my club, my community, my
country, and my world.

**4-H Motto:**

"To make the best better."

# CONTENTS

# INTRODUCTION

The following recipes were prepared by 4-H members who received outstanding-of-the-day recognition in the 4-H Food and Nutrition Show classes at The Ohio State Fair.

The recipes were not the only criterion by which winners were judged. 4-H members were judged on their understanding of their 4-H nutrition projects, the appearance of their table settings, the appearance of the final products, and the recipes. The Cooperative Extension Service and the Department of Human Nutrition and Food Management at The Ohio State University are not in a position to endorse or recommend any recipes used by 4-H members throughout the state. Recipes come from many sources and have not been tested by University faculty members.

Ideals Publishing Corp. has edited the recipes and taken the photographs. We hope you will enjoy your 4-H recipe book and also want you to know that profits from 4-H cookbook sales are being used to provide new opportunities and incentives for 4-H members and volunteer leaders throughout Ohio. Your support is very much appreciated.

We congratulate the 4-H members whose names appear with their recipes in this book. They have done an outstanding job in their 4-H projects and we commend them on their accomplishments.

ISBN 0-8249-0105-3

Copyright © MCMLXXXII by The Ohio 4-H Foundation
All rights reserved
Printed and bound in the United States of America
Published by Ideals Publishing Corporation
11315 Watertown Plank Road
Milwaukee, WI 53226

Pictured opposite:
Grilled German Potato Salad, page 4.

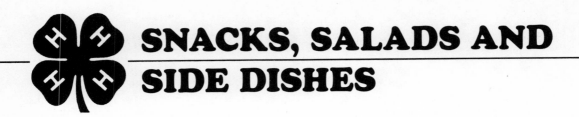

# SNACKS, SALADS AND SIDE DISHES

## CRISP VEGETABLE RELISHES

### Amy Brown
### Monroe County

**Cucumber Slices:**
Do not peel; run tines of fork down the cucumber. Do this on all sides, cutting through skin. Cut crosswise into thin slices.

**Radish Roses:**
Cut off top neatly. To make roses, make cuts down the side of red radishes close to the skin to make petals. Place in ice water to open.

**Celery Fans:**
Cut a stalk of celery into pieces 4 or 5 inches long. Cut ends of stalk into thin strips to make a fan. Put in ice water.

**Carrot Curls:**
Cut thin lengthwise strips of carrot. Roll up long slices and fasten with toothpicks. Chill in ice water to crisp.

## GRILLED GERMAN POTATO SALAD

### Rhoda Bowman
### Lucas County

5 unpared medium potatoes
1 cup finely chopped celery
8 slices bacon, fried crisp and crumbled

3 green onions (with tops) finely chopped (⅓ cup)

Cook potatoes in boiling salted water just until tender. Peel and cut into cubes (4 cups). In large bowl combine potatoes, celery, bacon, and onions.

**DRESSING**
½ cup mayonnaise or salad dressing
2 teaspoons sugar
1 teaspoon dry mustard

¼ cup white vinegar
1 teaspoon salt
¼ teaspoon coarsely ground pepper

Mix dressing ingredients and pour over potatoes; toss thoroughly. Place mixture on 18 × 13-inch sheet of heavy duty aluminum foil (double thickness); wrap securely. Place packet on grill 4 inches from coals. Cook 20 minutes; turn once.

## DEVILED EGGS

### Amy Brown
### Monroe County

| | |
|---|---|
| 6 eggs | ¾ teaspoon prepared mustard |
| 2 teaspoons vinegar | ½ teaspoon salt |
| 2 tablespoons salad dressing | ⅛ teaspoon ground pepper |

Fill a saucepan with water. Bring water to a boil. Lower 6 eggs into boiling water with a spoon. Bring water to simmer and simmer 20 to 25 minutes. Pour off hot water. Cool eggs in cold water at once. Peel cooked eggs. Cut eggs in half. Remove yolks from whites and mash yolks in bowl with fork. Add remaining ingredients. Pile yolk mixture back into whites. Sprinkle with paprika.

## V-8 VEGETABLE DIP

### Jenny Meeker
### Fulton County

| | |
|---|---|
| 1 8-ounce package cream cheese | ⅔ cup V-8 Juice |
| 1 teaspoon Italian salad dressing mix | |

Beat all ingredients until smooth. Serve with fresh vegetables.

## FRUIT SALAD PLATE

### Patty Neal
### Clermont County

| | |
|---|---|
| Head or leaf lettuce | One apple |
| Two oranges | One can (8 ounces) pineapple chunks |
| Two bananas | One-half pint cottage cheese |

Wash fruit and lettuce. Peel and section two oranges. Peel and slice two bananas. Core and slice the apple. DO NOT PEEL APPLE. Open pineapple can and save about one half of juice for fruit drinks. Pour the other half into a small dish. Coat the sliced bananas and apple with the pineapple juice to keep them from turning brown. Put lettuce on each salad plate. Spoon ¼-cup of cottage cheese on center of lettuce. Arrange orange sections, bananas, apple wedges, and pineapple chunks around cottage cheese to suit your design.

Serve as a light lunch or along with your dinner. Serves Four.

## SAUERKRAUT MIT ANANAS (PINEAPPLE SAUERKRAUT)

### Carol Paugstat
### Guernsey County

| | |
|---|---|
| 2 pounds fresh sauerkraut | 1½ to 2 pounds ripe pineapple |
| 5 cups unsweetened pineapple juice (2 20-ounce cans) | |

Drain the sauerkraut, wash it thoroughly under cold running water, and let it soak in a pot of cold water for 10 to 20 minutes, depending upon its acidity. A handful at a time, squeeze the sauerkraut until it is completely dry.

Combine the sauerkraut and pineapple juice in a heavy 3 to 4 quart saucepan, and bring to a boil over high heat, stirring with a fork to separate the sauerkraut strands. Reduce the heat to its lowest point and cover the pan tightly. Simmer, undisturbed, for 1½ to 2 hours, or until the sauerkraut has absorbed most of its cooking liquid.

With a long, sharp knife, cut the top 1½ inches off the pineapple and set the top aside. Hollow out the pineapple carefully, leaving ¼-inch layer of the fruit in the shell. Remove and discard the woody core of the hollowed-out fruit and cut the fruit into ½ inch cubes.

Stir the diced pineapple into the cooked sauerkraut, cook for a minute or two, then put the entire mixture into a large sieve set over a bowl. When all the liquid has drained through, pile the sauerkraut into the pineapple shell. Cover with the reserved pineapple top and serve on a large plate.

You can garnish around the pineapple with pineapple slices and put a crab apple in the hole.

## FRESH PINEAPPLE DIP

### Holly Hammerstrom
### Tuscarawas County

| | |
|---|---|
| 1 medium pineapple | 1 cup whipping cream, whipped |
| 1 egg, well beaten | Mint sprigs |
| 2 to 4 tablespoons sugar | Assorted fresh fruit |
| 1 teaspoon all-purpose flour | |

Cut a lengthwise slice from pineapple, removing about one-third of the pineapple. Scoop pulp from slice; discard rind. Scoop pulp from remaining portion of pineapple, leaving shell ½-inch thick; set shell aside.

Chop pineapple pulp into bite-size pieces, discarding core. Crush 1 cup of pineapple pieces; reserve remaining pineapple pieces for dipping.

Combine crushed pineapple (and juice that accumulates), egg, sugar and flour in a large saucepan. Cook over low heat until thickened; cool. Fold in whipped cream, and spoon into pineapple shell. Garnish with mint sprigs.

Serve dip with reserved pineapple pieces and other fresh fruit cut into serving pieces. Yield: about 3 cups.

## PARTY SANDWICH LOAF
### Laura Hester
### Huron County

### SHRIMP SALAD SPREAD
- 1 can (4½ ounces) tiny shrimp, rinsed and drained
- 1 hard-cooked egg, chopped
- 2 tablespoons celery, finely chopped
- 1 tablespoon lemon juice
- Dash of salt
- Dash of pepper
- 3 tablespoons salad dressing

Mix all above together.

### OLIVE-NUT SPREAD
- 1 package (3 ounces) cream cheese, softened
- ½ cup pecans, ground
- ¼ cup pimiento olives, chopped
- 2 tablespoons milk

Mix together.

### DEVILED HAM SPREAD
- 1 can (4½ ounces) deviled ham
- ¼ cup dairy sour cream
- 2 tablespoons sweet pickle relish, drained
- 1 tablespoon grated onion

Mix together

### FROSTING
- 2 packages (8 ounces each) cream cheese
- ½ cup of half and half

Trim crust from one loaf of unsliced bread. (I used a round loaf of my own homemade white bread, recipe follows.) Slice the loaf horizontally into 4 slices. Spread 3 of the 4 slices with soft butter or margarine.

Put the bottom slice on your serving plate. Spread the Shrimp filling evenly over that slice. Top with the next bread slice and spread on the Olive-Nut filling. Top with the third buttered slice and cover that with the Deviled Ham filling. The unbuttered slice is put on top.

Soften the cream cheese for the "frosting" and blend with the half and half. Frost the top and sides of the sandwich loaf. Decorate with slices of green and black olives or with vegetables of your choice. Refrigerate for at least 2½ hours. Garnish the platter with other vegetables. Slice to serve.

### MRS. KNOLL'S WHITE BREAD
- 4 cups very warm water
- 2 tablespoons dry yeast
- 2 tablespoons salt
- 4 tablespoons sugar
- 2 tablespoons oil
- 12 cups flour, approximately

Sprinkle yeast, salt, and sugar over warm water. Stir in 4 cups of the flour. Beat with wire whip. Stir in oil. Stir in 6 cups of flour and combine with wooden spoon. Knead on bread board until dough feels right—approximately 10 minutes. Be sure to flour the board; the bread will take up most of the 2 remaining cups of flour. Put dough in a well-greased bread bowl and allow to rise for about an hour until double in size. Poke down and turn on to board; shape into 4 loaves. Put into greased pans. Allow to rise about an hour until about double in size. Bake in 350°F oven for 45 minutes. One of the loaves can be made into a round loaf. Flatten slightly and place in a 12-inch greased pie pan or a 10-inch greased cake pan. Raise and bake as the others.

## THREE MEN IN A BOAT
### (Stuffed Baked Potatoes)

4 medium Idaho potatoes
¼ cup butter or margarine
¼ cup cream cheese
⅓ cup dairy sour cream (add more if needed)

2 tablespoons dried parsley or chives
Krazy Salt (to taste)
Dash paprika
½ cup shredded cheddar cheese

Preheat oven to 425°. Scrub potatoes gently with vegetable brush; pierce skins with fork. Bake about 1 hour or until tender. Cut potatoes in half lengthwise. Scoop out insides, being careful to leave skin intact on shell. With mixer beat potatoes with butter, cream cheese, sour cream, parsley, Krazy Salt, and paprika until smooth. Spoon mixture into shells. Sprinkle with shredded cheese. Reheat potatoes in oven until warm through and cheese is melted.

To make Three Men in a Boat; after removing potatoes from oven, thread slice of brick cheese onto a stick and stick into back part of potatoes for the sail. Put 3 mushroom caps on 3 toothpicks, and place in front of potato boat to represent 3 men. Serves 8.

In memory of Tana Homan, Mercer County.

## SEVEN-LAYERED SALAD

### Carolyn Cordial
### Delaware County

Lettuce
Tomatoes
Cucumbers
Walnuts

Cheese
Peas
Bacon bits

In a large bowl, place salad ingredients in layers. The amount used depends on how many people you are planning to serve. You can also add other items to your salad such as bean sprouts, ripe olives, etc., depending on your taste and the texture you want (crunchy, soft).

### DRESSING
¾ cup mayonnaise
1 tablespoon lemon juice
½ teaspoon salt
2 teaspoons parsley

½ cup sour cream
1 teaspoon mustard
2 tablespoons chopped green onion

Combine ingredients for dressing. Spread over salad and chill overnight. Make sure the dressing has totally sealed the salad so no air can get in, or the salad won't be as fresh.

Serve as a main dish or on the side.

## JAPANESE RICE BALLS

### Wendy Zech
### Franklin County

Prepare approximately 5 cups of short-grained, long-cooking rice according to package directions, omitting butter and salt. Be sure to overcook the rice so that it is very sticky. When rice is still fairly warm, but not too hot to handle, wet your hands, then sprinkle them with a thin layer of salt. Take a handful of rice and squeeze it tightly so that it is *very* tightly packed. Pack the rice for about a minute, then shape it into a medium ball. Press a small piece of canned tuna, a half of an olive, or a *small* cube of cucumber into the middle of the ball, and reshape it into either a ball or a three-dimensional half-circle. Do the same with the remaining rice. For variety, dried shark or seaweed can be sprinkled on top. These can be eaten hot or cold. Any rice balls containing meat should be refrigerated if not promptly eaten.

## CHEF'S SALAD

### Sharon Lamalie
### Sandusky County

1½ quarts salad greens, coarsely torn
1 cup sliced celery
1 cup sliced cucumber
½ cup green pepper strips
1 cup sliced carrots
1 cup cauliflower, broken in pieces
2 large tomatoes, cut in wedges
2 hard-cooked eggs, sliced
1 cup cheese strips
1½ cups cooked ham strips

In a large bowl, toss together salad greens, celery, cucumbers, green pepper, carrots, and cauliflower. (Salad greens should be crisp and dry.)

Arrange tomatoes, eggs, cheese and ham attractively on top of salad greens. Pass French dressing separately (recipe follows).

## FRENCH DRESSING

### Sharon Lamalie
### Sandusky County

1 cup salad oil
⅓ cup catsup
¾ cup sugar
¼ cup vinegar
1 tablespoon Worcestershire sauce

Put all ingredients into a blender. Blend at medium speed until thick. (½ cup chopped onion may be added when blended.) Refrigerate until used.

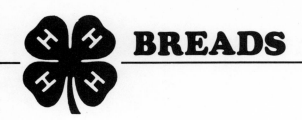 **BREADS**

# HOT CAKES WITH JAMS
# FOR A COOKOUT

## Suzanne Faldowski
## Jefferson County

2½ cups sifted flour      4 tablespoons shortening
 4 teaspoons baking powder      1 egg
 2 tablespoons sugar      2⅓ cups milk
 1 teaspoon salt

At home: sift dry ingredients together into bowl. Cut in shortening until mixture looks like meal. Put mixture into a bag to take to the cookout. Break egg into a quart container. Add milk.

At the cookout: Shake milk and egg until it is well mixed. Stir liquid into dry ingredients, beating only until it is well blended. Bake cakes on greased, moderately-hot griddle or skillet. Using a pancake turner, turn cakes over when golden brown on under side and bubbly on the top side. Finish baking. Turn only once. Do not press down on cakes with turner or you'll press out all the lightness.
    Serve hot from the griddle with jams.
    Yields approximately 30 three-inch cakes.

## RHUBARB JELLY
 5 cups of cut up rhubarb
2½ cups white sugar
 1 can (16 ounces) crushed pineapple
 1 box (6 ounces) of strawberry gelatin

Boil rhubarb, sugar, and pineapple for 20 minutes. Remove from heat. Add strawberry gelatin. Stir until it is dissolved, then put in jars. Keep in refrigerator.

## RASPBERRY JAM
 5 cups raspberries      4 cups sugar
 1 box fruit pectin

Place raspberries in large kettle. Stir pectin into prepared fruit. Bring to a full boil over high heat, stirring constantly. Stir in sugar all at once. Stir and bring to a full rolling boil. Then boil hard 1 minute stirring constantly. Remove from heat.
    Skim off foam with large metal spoon. Immediately ladle into hot jars leaving ¼ inch space at top. Cover jars with hot lids. Screw band on firmly. Place in boiling water bath for 5 minutes.

## RAISED CORNMEAL BREAD

### Susan Schrote
### Marion County

6½ to 7½ cups unsifted flour
1½ cups yellow corn meal
½ cup sugar
1 tablespoon salt
2 packages dry yeast

1½ cups milk
¾ cup water
½ cup margarine
2 eggs (at room temperature)
Melted margarine

In large bowl thoroughly mix 1½ cups flour, corn meal, sugar, salt, and undissolved yeast.

Combine milk, water, and ½ cup margarine in a saucepan. Heat over low heat until liquids are very warm (120° to 130° F.). Margarine does not need to melt. Gradually add to dry ingredients and beat 2 minutes at medium speed of electric mixer, scraping bowl occasionally. Add eggs and ½ cup flour. Beat at high speed 2 minutes, scraping bowl occasionally. Stir in enough additional flour to make a stiff dough. Turn out onto lightly floured board; knead until smooth and elastic, about 8 to 10 minutes. Place in greased bowl turning to grease top. Cover, let rise in warm place free from drafts until double in bulk, about 1 hour. Punch dough down; turn out onto lightly floured board. Cover, let rest on board 15 minutes. Divide dough into 3 equal pieces. Roll each to a 12 × 8-inch rectangle. Shape into loaves by rolling each piece with rolling pin, then beginning with upper short side roll toward you. Seal with thumb or heel of hand, seal ends, fold sealed ends under. Place seam-side down in 8½ × 4½ × 2½-inch loaf pans, cover; let rise in warm place, free from draft, until double in size, about 1 hour.

Bake at 375°F. about 30 to 35 minutes or until done. Remove from pans and cool on wire racks.

## THREE FLOUR BRAIDED BREAD

### Dottie DeWeese
### Shelby County

Combine 2¼ cups white flour, 2 teaspoons sugar, 1 teaspoon salt and 2 packages yeast. Add ¼ cup butter. Add 2¼ cups very warm water and beat with electric mixer 2 minutes at medium speed. Add 1 cup white flour. Beat at high speed 2 minutes. Divide into 3 bowls.

Make whole wheat dough by beating 2 tablespoons molasses and 1¼ cups whole wheat flour into ⅓ of batter. Make rye dough by adding 2 tablespoons molasses, 1 teaspoon caraway seed, 1 tablespoon cocoa and 1¼ cups rye flour into ⅓ of batter. Make white dough by beating 1¼ cups white flour into remaining batter.

Knead each dough until smooth and elastic, about 5 minutes.

Cover, let rise in warm place, about 1 hour. Punch down. On floured board, divide each into half, roll each piece into 15-inch rope. On greased baking sheet braid together, pinch ends to seal, let rise about 1 hour. Bake at 350°F. for 30 to 40 minutes or until done. Cool. Makes 2 loaves.

## WHOLE WHEAT BREAD

### Jean Skinner
### Hocking County

1 package active dry yeast *or* 1 cake compressed yeast
¼ cup of water
2½ cups hot water
½ cup brown sugar

3 teaspoons salt
¼ cup shortening
3 cups stirred whole-wheat flour
5 cups sifted all-purpose white flour

Soften active dry yeast in ¼ cup warm water (110°F.) or compressed yeast in ¼ cup lukewarm water (85°F.). Combine hot water, sugar, salt, and shortening; cool to lukewarm.

Stir in whole wheat flour and 1 cup of the white flour; beat well. Stir in softened yeast. Add enough of remaining flour to make a moderately stiff dough. Turn out on lightly floured surface; knead till smooth and satiny (10 to 12 minutes).

Shape dough into a ball; place in lightly greased bowl, turning once to grease surface. Cover; let rise in warm place until double (about 1½ hours). Punch down. Turn out on lightly floured surface again and knead for 3 minutes. Shape into ball; place in lightly greased bowl, turning once to grease surface. Cover; let rise until double. Punch down. Cut in two portions; shape each into smooth ball. Cover and let rest 10 minutes.

Shape into loaves; place in greased 8½ × 4½ × 2½-inch loaf dishes. Let rise until double (about 1¼ hours). Bake in moderate oven (375°F.) about 45 minutes. Cover with foil last 20 minutes, if necessary. Makes 2 loaves.

## WHOLE WHEAT BREAD

### Lynn Settlemyre
### Clinton County

¾ cup milk
3 tablespoons sugar
4 teaspoons salt
⅓ cup margarine
⅓ cup molasses

1½ cups warm water
2 packages or cakes yeast
2¾ cups white flour
4½ cups whole wheat flour

Scald milk; stir in sugar, salt, margarine, and molasses and cool. Put water into large bowl and sprinkle yeast over it; stir. Add milk mixture, 2 cups white flour and 2 cups wheat flour. Beat until smooth. Add enough flour to make a soft dough; turn onto board and knead until smooth and elastic. Place in greased bowl and cover; let rise in warm place. Shape loaves and place in greased 9 × 5 × 3-inch pans. Let rise again until doubled in bulk.

Bake 25-30 minutes in 400° oven. Remove from pans and cool. Makes 2 loaves.

### SIXTY-MINUTE ROLLS

**Martha Kuder**
**Seneca County**

3½ to 4½ cups unsifted flour
3 tablespoons sugar
1 teaspoon salt
2 packages yeast

1 cup milk
½ cup water
¼ cup butter

In bowl mix 1½ cups flour, sugar, salt, and undissolved yeast. Combine milk, water, and butter in saucepan. Heat over low heat until liquids are warm (120° - 130°F.). Butter does not need to melt. Gradually add to dry ingredients and beat for 2 minutes at medium speed of electric mixer. Add ½ cup flour. Beat at high speed for 2 minutes. Stir in enough additional flour to make a soft dough. Turn out onto a lightly floured board; knead until smooth and elastic, about 5 minutes. Place in greased bowl, turning to grease top. Cover; place bowl in pan of hot water. Let rise 15 minutes. Turn dough out onto floured board. Divide in half and shape into rolls. Cover; let rise in warm place, 15 minutes. Bake at 425°F. about 12 minutes or until done. Remove from baking sheets and cool on wire rack.

### REFRIGERATOR ROLLS

**Cindy Johns**
**Erie County**

2 packages active dry yeast
1 cup water
1 teaspoon sugar
2 cups milk, scalded
¾ cup melted margarine

¾ cup sugar
4 teaspoons salt
2 beaten eggs
10 to 11 cups flour

Soften active dry yeast in warm water (110°F.); add 1 teaspoon sugar to yeast mixture. Add milk, cooled to lukewarm, margarine, ¾ cup sugar, and salt.

Add eggs; beat well. Add flour to make soft dough; let stand 10 minutes; knead on lightly floured surface till smooth and elastic. Place in greased bowl, turning once to grease surface, and cover; store in refrigerator.

Shape rolls about 2 hours before serving. Let rise till double in bulk. Bake in hot oven (425°F.) 15 to 20 minutes.

Punch down unused dough and return to refrigerator.

Makes 4 to 5 dozen medium rolls.

## COUNTRY CRUST BREAD

### Marcia Stuckey
### Fulton County

2 packages active dry yeast
2 cups warm water (105° to 115°)
½ cup sugar
1 tablespoon salt

2 eggs
¼ cup vegetable oil
6 to 6½ cups bread flour
Margarine or butter, softened

Dissolve yeast in warm water in large mixing bowl, stir in sugar, salt, eggs, ¼ cup oil, and 3 cups of the flour. Beat until smooth. Mix in enough remaining flour to make dough easy to handle. Turn dough onto lightly floured surface; knead until smooth and elastic, 8 to 10 minutes. Place in greased bowl; turn greased side up. (At this time, dough may be refrigerated 3 to 4 days.) Cover; let rise in warm place until double, about 1 hour. Punch down dough; divide into halves. Roll each half into a rectangle 18 × 9 inches. Roll tightly beginning at 9 inch side. Press with thumbs to seal after each turn. Pinch edge firmly to seal. Press each end with side of hand to seal, fold ends under. Place loaf, seam side down, in greased 9 × 5 × 3 inch baking pan. Brush with oil. Let rise till double about 1 hour. Heat oven to 375°. Bake until loaves are deep golden brown and sound hollow when tapped, 30-35 minutes. Remove from pans. Brush with margarine, cool on wire rack. Makes 2 loaves.

## CLOVERLEAF ROLLS

### Bonnie Wittes
### Lucas County

4½ to 5 cups flour
2 packages active dry yeast
1 cup milk
½ cup shortening

½ cup sugar
2 teaspoons salt
3 eggs

In large bowl combine 2 cups flour and yeast. In saucepan heat milk, shortening, sugar, and salt till warm (115° to 120°F.), stirring constantly to melt shortening. Add to dry mixture. Add eggs. Beat at low speed with electric mixer for ½ minute, scraping sides of bowl; then beat on high for 3 minutes. By hand stir in enough remaining flour to make moderately stiff dough. Turn out on a lightly floured surface. Knead till smooth (5 to 8 minutes). Shape into ball. Place in greased bowl. Turn once. Cover. Let rise until double, 1 to 1½ hours.

Punch down dough. Turn out on floured surface. Cover. Let rest 10 minutes. Shape into rolls. Cover, let rise till double (30 to 45 minutes). Bake at 400°F. until done, 10 to 12 minutes. Remove from pans. Makes 2 to 3 dozen rolls.

## WHITE BREAD

### Carla Ricketts
### Fairfield County

5½ to 6½ cups all-purpose flour*
3 tablespoons sugar
2 teaspoons salt
1 package active dry yeast

1½ cups water
½ cup milk
3 tablespoons margarine

In a large bowl thoroughly mix 2 cups flour, sugar, salt and *undissolved* yeast.

Combine water, milk, and margarine in saucepan. Heat over low heat until liquids are warm (margarine does not need to melt). Gradually add to dry ingredients and beat 2 minutes with electric mixer at medium speed, scraping bowl occasionally. Add ¾ cup flour, or enough to make a thick batter. Beat at high speed for 2 minutes, scraping bowl occasionally.

Stir in enough remaining flour with spoon to make a soft dough. Turn out onto lightly floured board and knead until smooth and elastic, about 8-10 minutes.

Place in greased bowl; turn dough over to grease top. Cover; let rise in warm place free from draft until doubled, about 1 hour.

Punch down dough; turn onto lightly floured board. Cover and let rest for 15 minutes. Divide dough in half; shape each half into a loaf. Place in greased 8½ × 4½ × 2½-inch loaf pans. Cover; let rise in warm place free from draft until doubled, about 1 hour.

Bake in a hot oven (400°F.) for 25 to 30 minutes, or until done. Remove from pans and cool on wire racks. Makes 2 loaves.

* Bread flour does work better.

## WHOLE WHEAT BREAD

### Dottie DeWeese
### Shelby County

5½ to 6 cups white flour
2 cups whole wheat flour
3 tablespoons sugar
4 teaspoons salt
2 packages dry yeast

2 cups milk
¾ cup water
¼ cup margarine
¼ cup molasses

Combine two kinds of flour in large bowl. Thoroughly mix 2½ cups flour mixture, sugar, salt and undissolved yeast. Combine milk, water, margarine and molasses, gradually add to dry ingredients; beat 2 minutes. Add 1 cup flour mixture; beat at high speed for 2 minutes. Stir in enough additional flour to make a stiff dough. Turn onto a floured board and knead 8 to 10 minutes. Let rest 20 minutes. Shape and let rise for about 1 hour.

Bake at 400°F. about 40 minutes. Makes two loaves.

# IRISH SODA BREAD

## Jean Moats
## Madison County

| | |
|---|---|
| 2¼ to 2¾ cups unsifted flour | 1 package yeast |
| 3 tablespoons sugar | 1 cup buttermilk |
| ½ teaspoon salt | 2 tablespoons margarine |
| 1 tablespoon caraway seed | ¾ cup raisins |
| ½ teaspoon baking soda | |

In a small mixer bowl thoroughly mix 1 cup flour, sugar, salt, caraway seed, baking soda and undissolved dry yeast.

Combine buttermilk and margarine in a saucepan. Heat over low heat until liquid is very warm (120° to 130°F.). Gradually add to dry ingredients and beat 2 minutes at medium speed of electric mixer. Add ¼ cup flour. Beat at high speed 2 minutes. Stir in raisins and enough additional flour to make a soft dough. Cover bowl; let rise in warm place until doubled in bulk, about 50 minutes.

Punch dough down. Turn out onto lightly floured board. Knead 20 times, forming a smooth round ball. Place in a greased casserole. Cover; let rise until doubled about 50 minutes.

Cut a shallow cross on top just before baking. Bake at 350°F. about 30 minutes. Remove from casserole and cool on a wire rack. Makes 1 loaf.

# PEBBLE-TOP OATMEAL BREAD

## Gina Sandlin
## Lucas County

| | |
|---|---|
| 1 package active dry yeast | 2½ cups regular or quick-cooking rolled oats |
| ¼ cup warm water (about 110°F.) | 1 cup each boiling water & cold water |
| ¼ cup molasses | 4½ to 5 cups all-purpose flour, unsifted |
| ¼ cup butter or margarine | 3 tablespoons milk |
| 2 teaspoons salt | |
| ¼ cup firmly packed brown sugar | |

In a small bowl, combine yeast, warm water, and 1 tablespoon of the molasses; let stand until bubbly (about 15 minutes). In a large bowl, combine butter, remaining molasses, salt, sugar, 2 cups of the oats, and boiling water; stir until butter melts; add cold water and yeast mixture. Beat in 4 cups of the flour, 1 cup at a time.

Turn dough out onto a floured board; knead until smooth and elastic (10 to 20 minutes), adding flour as needed to prevent sticking. Turn dough over in a greased bowl; cover and let rise in a warm place until doubled (about 1 hour).

Punch dough down; knead briefly on a lightly floured board to release air. Divide in half and shape each half into a loaf; place in greased 9 × 5-inch loaf pans. Soften remaining rolled oats in milk; dot over tops. Cover, let rise in a warm place until doubled (about 45 minutes).

Bake in a 350°F. oven for about 1 hour or until bread sounds hollow when tapped. Turn out on a rack to cool. Makes 2 loaves.

## YEAST ROLLS

### Darla Blackburn
### Morgan County

| | |
|---|---|
| 1 package active dry yeast | ¼ cup sugar |
| ¼ cup warm water (about 110°F) | 1¼ teaspoons salt |
| 1 cup hot milk | 1 egg |
| ¼ cup shortening or oil | About 4 cups flour |

Dissolve yeast in water. Mix milk, fat, sugar, and salt in a large bowl. Cool until lukewarm. Stir in egg and yeast. Add 2 cups flour and beat until smooth. Gradually stir in more flour until dough leaves sides of bowl.

Turn dough out onto lightly floured surface and knead dough until smooth and elastic.

Place in a lightly greased bowl and turn over once to grease upper side of dough. Cover and let rise in a warm place (80° to 85° F.) until almost double in bulk, 1 to 1¼ hours. Dough should rise until a light touch leaves a slight depression. Press the dough down into the bowl to remove air bubbles.

To make plain rolls, divide dough into small pieces and roll into balls about 1½ inch in diameter. Place in a shallow greased pan with sides touching.

Cover loosely and let rise in a warm place until double in bulk, 45 minutes to 1 hour.

Bake at 400°F 15 to 20 minutes. Brush rolls with melted butter or margarine after removing them from the oven. Makes 18 to 24 rolls.

## WHITE BREAD

### Kelly Gahn
### Sandusky County

| | |
|---|---|
| 2¼ cups lukewarm liquid (milk or water) | 2 cakes compressed yeast |
| 1 tablespoon salt | 2 tablespoons shortening |
| 3 tablespoons sugar | 7 to 7½ cups sifted flour |

Mix liquid, salt and sugar together in a large bowl. Crumble yeast into mixture; add shortening. Mixing first with a spoon, then with hands, gradually add flour

After dough leaves sides of bowl, put it out on a lightly floured board. Knead until satin smooth (approximately 10 minutes). Place in greased bowl. Turn dough over so the top will be greased. Let rise until double in volume. Punch down and let rise until almost double in bulk (approximately 45 minutes). Divide dough into two portions, let rest 10 minutes. Mold dough into loaf shapes and put into greased loaf pans. Let dough rise in pans until the dough is even with the sides of the pan and the middle is nicely rounded. Bake at 425° degrees for 25 to 30 minutes, or until loaf sounds hollow when lightly tapped. Remove from pan immediately and allow to cool on rack. Top may be brushed with melted butter if desired. This will make a soft crust.

## QUICHE PASTRY

**Joanne Choma**
**Columbiana County**

| | |
|---|---|
| 3 cups flour | 1 egg, separated |
| 1 teaspoon salt | ⅓ cup water |
| 1 cup shortening | |

Stir together flour and salt. Cut in shortening until crumbs are the size of small peas. Beat egg yolk with water and sprinkle into flour a little at a time, mixing lightly, until dough begins to stick together. Wrap and chill 15 minutes. Divide dough in half. Roll each portion ⅛ inch thick. Fit gently into ungreased 10-inch pie pan. Trim pastry and brush with beaten egg white. Bake in 450°F. oven 5 to 8 minutes or until golden.

Add Quiche filling as directed.

Makes enough for 2 pies.

## QUICHE LORRAINE

**Joanne Choma**
**Columbiana County**

| | |
|---|---|
| ½ pound bacon (10-12 slices) | 1 large prebaked pie shell |
| 4 eggs | ¼ pound cheddar cheese, grated |
| 2 cups cream | ¼ pound Swiss cheese, grated |
| Pinch sugar | |
| Pinch cayenne pepper | |
| 1 teaspoon salt | |
| Pinch nutmeg | |
| Pinch black pepper | |

Cook bacon until crisp and break into small pieces. Beat eggs, cream and seasonings long enough to mix thoroughly. Rub a little butter over the surface of the pie shell. Sprinkle bacon on the bottom, then cheeses. Pour egg mixture over the cheese.

Bake at 375°F. for 40-45 minutes, or until eggs are set and knife blade inserted comes out clean. Allow to cool slightly before cutting.

## MINI STUFFED BURGERS

### Leslie Breyley
### Crawford County

| | |
|---|---|
| 2 pounds ground beef | 1 diced tomato |
| 1 egg | ½ red onion, diced |
| 2 tablespoons mustard | ½ cup diced pickles |
| ¾ cup crushed taco-flavored chips | 1 cup shredded cheese |
| 2 tablespoons Worcestershire sauce | 1 can mushrooms, diced |
| ½ teaspoon salt | ¼ cup melted butter |
| ¼ teaspoon pepper | 1 tablespoon chili powder |

Place ground beef, egg, mustard, crushed taco chips, Worcestershire sauce, salt and pepper in a large bowl, and mix thoroughly.

Divide meat into 12 balls. Press into patties. Make 6 larger patties, about 7 inches in diameter, and 6 smaller patties, about 5 inches in diameter. On the larger patties, layer tomato, onion, pickles, cheese and mushrooms. Place a smaller patty on top and press edges together very tightly. Grill for 5 to 6 minutes on each side. Baste with butter mixed with chili powder. Serve on a bun with lettuce, catsup, and mustard.

## TAMALE LOAF

### Sue Smalley
### Highland County

| | |
|---|---|
| 2 tablespoons oil | 1 tablespoon chili powder |
| 1 large onion, chopped | 1 No. 2½ can tomatoes (3½ cups) |
| 1 clove garlic, minced | 1 cup yellow corn meal |
| 1 small green pepper, chopped | 1 cup milk |
| 1 cup chopped celery | 1 No. 2 can cream-style corn |
| 1 pound ground beef | ½ cup grated American cheese |
| 2 teaspoons salt | Pitted ripe olives |

Cook onion, garlic, green pepper and celery in oil for 5 minutes.

Add ground meat and cook until lightly browned, stirring often. Add salt, chili powder and tomatoes and cook 15 minutes.

Mix corn meal with milk and stir into meat mixture. Cook 15 minutes longer, stirring constantly. Add cream-style corn.

Pour into greased pan; top with grated cheese, and decorate with olives. Bake in preheated 325° F. oven one hour. Makes 6 generous servings.

## TEXAS BARBECUE

### Janelle Meredith
### Fayette County

Pork loin roast (2½ pounds)
SAUCE:
⅓ cup corn oil
⅓ cup chopped onion
½ cup light corn syrup, minus 2 tablespoons
2 tablespoons dark molasses
¼ cup water

½ cup ketchup
¼ cup lemon juice
⅓ cup vinegar
2 tablespoons prepared mustard
2 tablespoons Worcestershire sauce
1 teaspoon hickory salt
½ teaspoon pepper

Roast pork loin at 325°F. for 1½ hours in a tightly covered baking pan. Do not add liquid. Finish cooking on a medium hot charcoal grill for 45 minutes until the meat is browned and smoked through. It should be turned frequently. Slice thinly and serve with heated barbecue sauce. To prepare sauce, heat corn oil in a heavy pan. Add onion and cook till tender on low heat. Add remaining ingredients. Turn up heat and let sauce boil, stirring often, for 5 minutes. Simmer 10 more minutes.

## CORNED BEEF CASSEROLE

### Rhea Ann Lahmers
### Tuscarawas County

8 ounces noodles
4 tablespoons margarine
1 medium size onion, chopped
1 medium green pepper, chopped
1 can (12 ounces) corned beef, shredded
10½ ounce can condensed cheddar cheese soup

10½ ounce can condensed cream of chicken soup
1 cup milk
½ cup soft, stale bread crumbs or cracker crumbs

Cook 8 ounces of noodles in 3 quarts of water with 1 tablespoon of salt for 8-10 minutes. Drain. Melt 4 tablespoons margarine in frying pan; remove 2 tablespoons and reserve for topping. Fry chopped onion and green pepper. Add corned beef, cheese and chicken soups, milk and noodles. Mix gently. Pour mixture into baking dish or pan. Mix crumbs and 2 tablespoons melted margarine in a bowl. Sprinkle on top of mixture. Bake in 350°F. oven about 1 hour. The crumbs should turn brown. Garnish with cheddar cheese and pepper.

## HUNGRY HAM RINGS

### Leeanna Engle
### Highland County

1½ pounds ground ham
½ pound ground pork
1½ cups bread crumbs
1 cup milk

2 eggs
1 No. 2½ can pineapple slices
Maraschino cherries

Mix together ham, pork, crumbs, milk and eggs; roll into doughnut shapes. Place a pineapple slice and a cherry between two ham rings, reserving pineapple juice. Grill 1¼ hours (plus or minus) on foil, basting often with sauce.

### SAUCE

1½ cups brown sugar
½ cup pineapple juice
1 teaspoon dry mustard

½ cup vinegar
1 teaspoon Worcestershire sauce

Bring all ingredients to a boil.

## GINGER GLAZED SPARERIBS

### Dan Kraner
### Van Wert County

5 pounds pork spareribs
½ cup sugar
1 tablespoon cornstarch
1 teaspoon salt
¼ teaspoon ground pepper

½ teaspoon ground ginger
⅓ cup lemon juice
¼ cup soy sauce
¼ cup water

Place ribs in a 6 quart Dutch oven. Add enough water to cover. Cook over high heat till mixture comes to a boil. Reduce heat to low and simmer 45 minutes or until tender. Drain set aside.

Combine sugar, cornstarch, salt, pepper, ginger, lemon juice, soy sauce and water in a 2 quart sauce pan. Bring this to a boil for 5 minutes. Remove from heat.

Grill ribs 4 inches from gray charcoals, turning and basting with glaze often. Cook 20 minutes, or until glazed and nicely browned. Makes 3 servings.

Serve with: Vegetable kabobs, warm buttered biscuits, fruit basket and a tall glass of cold milk.

Ginger Glazed Spareribs

## FLOUR TORTILLAS

**Rhonda Bush**
**Richland County**

2 cups all purpose flour
1 teaspoon salt
1 teaspoon baking powder

1 tablespoon lard or shortening
½ to ¾ cup warm water (110°)

In mixing bowl stir together flour, salt, and baking powder. Cut in lard till mixture resembles corn meal. Add ½ cup warm water and mix till dough can be gathered into a ball (if needed, add more water, 1 tablespoon at a time). Let dough rest 15 minutes. Divide dough into 12 portions; shape into balls. On a lightly floured surface, roll each ball to a 7-inch round. Trim uneven edges to make round tortillas.
Prepare Enchilada filling.

## ENCHILADAS

**Rhonda Bush**
**Richland County**

1 pound ground beef
1 onion, chopped
1 tablespoon chili powder
1 teaspoon salt
¼ teaspoon garlic powder

1 can (8 ounces) tomato sauce
2 cups grated cheddar or Monterey Jack cheese
1 can (10 ounces) enchilada sauce

Brown meat with onion. Drain off fat and add chili powder, salt, garlic powder and tomato sauce; mix and heat well. Lightly fry each tortilla in ½ inch medium hot oil. Drain on paper towels. Fill each tortilla with 2 heaping tablespoons of the meat mixture. Roll tortilla closed, placing seam side down in an 8 inch × 12 inch baking dish. Pour enchilada sauce over tortillas and top with grated cheese. Bake, uncovered, at 350°F. for 15-20 minutes.

## SMOKED SAUSAGE AND DRIED GREEN BEANS SUPREME

**Christine Lauer**
**Tuscarawas County**

Place 3 cups dried green beans in saucepan. Add 6 cups hot water. Place lid on pan and let stand 2½ hours. Add ½ teaspoon salt and 1 pound smoked sausage cut in 2 inch pieces. Place lid on pan; simmer for 20-30 minutes. Add a little water if needed. Serves 4.

## WESTERN CHILI CASSEROLE

### Lisa Rammel
### Miami County

1 pound ground beef
1 cup chopped onion
¼ cup chopped celery
1 can (15 ounces) chili con carne with beans

¼ teaspoon pepper
2 cups corn chips, slightly crushed
1 cup shredded, sharp process cheese

Brown meat; add ¾ cup of onion and the celery; cook until just tender. Drain off excess fat. Add chili and pepper; heat. Place layer of chips in ungreased 1½ quart casserole. Alternate layers of chili mixture, chips and cheese, reserving ½ cup chips and ¼ cup cheese. Sprinkle center with reserved ¼ cup cheese and ¼ cup onion.

Cover and bake at 350° for 10 minutes or until hot through. To serve, sprinkle reserved ½ cup chips around border of casserole. Makes 6 servings.

## MEAT LOAF

### Jami Sadler
### Scioto County

1¼ pounds ground beef
¼ pound ground pork
3 slices bread, torn
1 egg, beaten
¼ teaspoon salt

¼ cup chopped onion
¾ cup reconstituted dried milk
1 teaspoon salt
¼ teaspoon pepper
¼ cup chopped green pepper

Mix all ingredients thoroughly. Place in a loaf pan. Bake uncovered at 350°F. about 1 hour. OPTIONAL: Before baking, spread with ¼ cup catsup or barbecue sauce.

## MEAT LOAF MARUEL

### Jami Sadler
### Scioto County

Hot baked meat loaf
4 cups instant potatoes
2 slightly beaten eggs

Melted cheddar cheese
Decorator bag and coupler
Tubes 32, 104, 352, 3, 225

Prepare potatoes using a little less liquid than the package calls for so potatoes are stiff. Beat in eggs. Frost entire meat loaf with potatoes, reserving some for decoration. Add melted cheese to reserved potatoes. Place in decorator bag and decorate frosted loaf. Use tube 32 for the border, 104 for rose buds, 352 for leaves, 3 for stems and 225 for drop flowers.

Return to 500° oven for about 10-15 minutes or until potatoes are golden brown.

## POOR BOY'S FILETS

### Darcy Miller
### Holmes County

5 slices bacon
1 pound lean ground beef
Seasoning salt
Lemon pepper
¼ cup grated Parmesan cheese

1 (2-ounce) can of mushroom slices, drained
3 tablespoons finely chopped olives
2 tablespoons finely chopped onion
2 tablespooons finely chopped green pepper

In a skillet, partially cook bacon. Drain on paper toweling. Pat ground beef on waxed paper into a 12 × 7½ × ¼-inch rectangle. Sprinkle lightly with salt and lemon pepper. Top with Parmesan cheese. Combine mushrooms, olives, onion and green pepper; sprinkle evenly over meat. Starting from short end, roll up jelly roll fashion, using the waxed paper to roll. Cut into five 1½-inch slices. Wrap each slice with strip of bacon, securing with wooden picks. Grill or broil on medium coals eight minutes per side.

## APPLE-ORANGE STUFFED PORK CHOPS

### Darlene Haegele
### Licking County

6 pork loin chops (1½ inches thick)
½ cup chopped celery
½ cup chopped, unpeeled apple
2 tablespoons butter
1 beaten egg

1½ cups toasted raisin bread cubes
½ teaspoon grated orange peel
1 orange, sectioned and peeled
¼ teaspoon salt
⅛ teaspoon ground cinnamon

Make a slit in each chop cutting from fat side almost to bone. Season cavity with salt and pepper. In small saucepan, cook celery and apple in butter until tender, but not brown. Combine egg, bread cubes, orange peel, chopped orange, salt, and cinnamon. Pour cooked celery and apple over bread cube mixture; toss lightly. Spoon about ¼ cup stuffing into each pork chop. Securely fasten pocket opening with wooden picks.

Grill chops over medium coals about 20 minutes. Turn meat and grill till done, 15 to 20 minutes more. Before serving, remove the picks.

Apple-Orange Stuffed Pork Chops

## BAKED HAM

2 tablespoons Kitchen Bouquet
½ cup soy sauce
¼ cup prepared mustard
¼ cup brown sugar

10 pound sugar cured ham, precooked

Put ham in roasting pan. Mix remaining ingredients together; brush over ham. Cover and bake at 250° for 1 hour or until hot through.

## SAUERBRATEN
### (German Pot Roast)

**Tammy Pfaff**
**Crawford County**

3 bay leaves
6 whole cloves
2 cups wine or cider vinegar
2 cups water
2 onions, peeled and sliced
½ teaspoon black pepper
2 tablespoons sugar
¼ cup fat

4 pounds boneless beef pot roast

Place meat in a large, deep bowl. Place remaining ingredients, except fat, in a saucepan and bring to a boil. Pour over meat. Cover and refrigerate 48 hours or more, turning meat several times to season evenly. Remove meat, reserving marinade. Dry meat well with paper towels. Heat fat in a heavy saucepan or Dutch oven over medium heat. Brown meat well on all sides. Strain marinade and add 1 cup to meat. Reserve remaining marinade. Cover and cook meat over low heat until fork-tender (about 1½ hours). Add more marinade, if necessary, to keep ½ inch liquid in the pan. Remove meat to a warm platter, slice and serve. Makes 10 to 12 servings.

To Make Gravy (Saft): Thicken liquid with a thin flour and water paste. Allow 1½ tablespoons flour for each cup of liquid. Add more marinade or water for the desired flavor and consistency. Cook to thicken and blend flavors. Check seasonings. Strain, if necessary. Pour part of the gravy over meat and pass the rest.

## ENCHILADAS DE POLLO
### (Chicken or Turkey Enchiladas)

### Jan Knight
### Logan County

1 can (16 ounces) tomatoes
1 can (4 ounces) green chili peppers, rinsed and seeded
½ teaspoon coriander seed
½ teaspoon salt
1 cup dairy sour cream
2 cups cooked chicken or turkey, finely chopped
1 package (3 ounces) cream cheese, softened
¼ cup onion, finely chopped
¾ teaspoon salt
2 tablespoons cooking oil
12 6-inch tortillas
1 cup (4 ounces) shredded Monterey Jack cheese
½ cup shredded Colby cheese, optional

Place undrained tomatoes, chili peppers, coriander seed, and the ½ teaspoon salt in blender container. Cover; blend until mixture is smooth. Add sour cream; cover and blend just until combined. Set aside.

Combine chicken or turkey, cream cheese, onion and ¾ teaspoon salt. In a skillet, heat cooking oil. Dip tortillas, one at a time, into hot oil for 10 seconds or just until limp. Drain on paper toweling. Spoon chicken mixture on tortillas; roll up. Place seam side down in 12 × 7½ × 2-inch baking dish. Pour tomato mixture over. Cover with foil; bake in 350°F. oven about 30 minutes or until heated through. Remove foil; sprinkle with shredded cheese, putting Monterey Jack cheese down the middle and Colby around the outside to give a pleasing appearance. Return to oven until cheese is melted. Makes 6 servings.

## CORNED BEEF CASSEROLE

### Samantha Jordan
### Preble County

8 ounces noodles
2 tablespoons margarine
1 medium sized onion chopped
1 stalk of celery, cleaned and chopped
1 can (12 ounces) corned beef, shredded
1 can (10 ounces) condensed cream of chicken soup
1 can (10 ounces) condensed cheddar cheese soup
1 package slivered almonds
4 ounces shredded cheddar cheese

Cook noodles in water for 8-10 minutes. Drain. Melt margarine in frying pan. Fry chopped onion and chopped celery. Then add corned beef. Add soups and drained noodles. Mix.

Pour mixture into baking dish. Bake 30-40 minutes at 350° F.

Add almonds and shredded cheddar cheese to the top when almost done, just long enough for cheese to melt.

## FINNISH MEATBALLS

### Jean Scholz
### Montgomery County

1½ pounds hamburger
1 egg, slightly beaten
2 teaspoons salt
½ teaspoon pepper
½ teaspoon dill weed
2 cups grated raw potato
½ cup finely chopped onion

½ cup finely chopped green pepper
1 to 2 tablespoons butter
1 can (8 ounces) tomato sauce
⅓ cup cold water
1 tablespoon flour
1 cup dairy sour cream

In a mixing bowl, lightly blend meat, egg, and a mixture of the seasonings and vegetables. Lightly shape into 1 inch balls. (Rinse hands often in cold water, or use a meatballer). Brown meatballs evenly on all sides in hot butter in a large skillet. When thoroughly cooked, remove meatballs to a warm serving dish; set aside, and keep hot.

Add tomato sauce to the drippings in the skillet and stir in a blend of water and flour. Bring rapidly to boiling, stirring mixture constantly. Cook 1 to 2 minutes. Reduce heat. Stirring gravy vigorously with a whip or spoon, add sour cream a small amount at a time. Heat thoroughly, about 3 minutes; do not boil. Pour gravy over meatballs and serve. Makes about 6 dozen meatballs.

## SPAGHETTI WITH MEAT SAUCE

### Laura Heckman
### Lucas County

1 pound ground beef
1 medium-sized onion, finely chopped
1 clove garlic, minced (optional)
½ teaspoon oregano (optional)
1 teaspoon salt
¼ teaspoon pepper
1 can tomato paste

### Lora Satterthwaite
### Clinton County

1 can tomato sauce
1 cup water
1 bay leaf (optional)
8 ounces uncooked spaghetti
½ cup grated Parmesan, Romano or other cheese

Crumble ground beef into 4-quart saucepan. Add onion, garlic, oregano, salt and pepper. Heat to brown meat.

Add tomato paste, tomato sauce, water and bay leaf. Bring to a boil, then simmer, uncovered, over low heat about 45 minutes.

While sauce is simmering, cook spaghetti. Drain and rinse.

Place hot spaghetti on a platter. Cover with meat sauce. Sprinkle with cheese.

## CHICKEN NAVARESA

### Laurie Kreuz
### Fulton County

1 roasting chicken, 3 to 4 pounds
¼ cup olive oil
1 pound small white onions, peeled
1 pound carrots, pared and cut into quarters

1 cup white wine
1½ teaspoons flour
½ teaspoon salt
⅛ teaspoon pepper
Rice

Preheat oven to 350°F. Wash chicken under cold water; dry on paper towels. Tie ends of legs together with twine. Bend wings under body of chicken. Slowly heat olive oil in large Dutch oven. Sauté chicken, breast side down, until golden-brown. Turn breast side up. Roast, uncovered, in preheated oven, 15 minutes.

Arrange onions around chicken; then baste onions and chicken with pan drippings. Roast 15 minutes longer.

Remove from oven. Place carrots under chicken; pour white wine over it. Roast covered, 1 to 1½ hours, or until chicken and vegetables are fork-tender.

Remove chicken to warm platter; surround with vegetables. Keep warm.

Measure liquid in Dutch oven; if necessary, add water to measure one cup. In small saucepan, combine liquid, flour, salt, and pepper; bring to boiling, stirring constantly. Reduce heat, and simmer 1 minute. Serve sauce with chicken and vegetables.

Cook rice according to package directions and arrange it on platter. Place chicken and vegetables in an attractive manner on top of the rice. Serve while hot.

## FONDULOHA

### Debra Denier
### Clinton County

2 fresh pineapples
2½ cups cut-up cooked chicken or turkey
¾ cup diced celery
¾ cup mayonnaise
2 tablespoons chopped chutney
1 teaspoon curry powder

1 medium banana, sliced
⅓ cup salted peanuts
½ cup flaked coconut
1 can (11 ounces) mandarin orange segments, drained
Green pepper strips

Select pineapples with fresh green leaves. Cut each pineapple lengthwise in half through green top. Remove fruit by cutting along edges with curved knife. Cut fruit into cubes, removing eyes and fiberous core. Drain pineapple shells, cut side down.

Combine cubed pineapple, the chicken and celery; cover and chill. Mix mayonnaise, chutney and curry powder. Cover and chill. Just before serving, drain fruit mixture. Toss lightly with mayonnaise mixture, banana and peanuts; fill pineapple shells. Sprinkle with coconut and garnish with mandarin orange segments and green pepper strips.

## SATAY AND PEANUT SAUCE
### (For Chicken, Pork or Beef)

### Teri Bennett
### Clinton County

**SATAY MARINADE**
Chicken, pork, or beef
½ cup soy sauce
2 cloves of garlic, crushed

3 tablespoons brown sugar
3 green onions, chopped

**PEANUT SAUCE (FOR SATAY)**
1 tablespoon salad oil
2 tablespoons finely chopped green onion
Dash of minced garlic
½ teaspoon fresh ginger root
1 tablespoon brown sugar

½ cup chunk style peanut butter
¼ cup water
2 teaspoons soy sauce
½ cup coconut milk
Hot sauce to taste.

Cut meat into ½-inch chunks and put on bamboo sticks. Mix together soy sauce, garlic, brown sugar, and onions. Use to marinate meat at room temperature for 1½ to 2 hours. Grill or fry until brown.

Sauté onion, garlic and ginger root in oil. Add remaining ingredients and simmer until sauce thickens a bit. If sauce is too thick, add a little more water.

## SAUSAGE SPAGHETTI

### Diana Bahnsen
### Ottawa County

1 pound smoked sausage, cut into 1-inch slices
1 green pepper, diced
2 medium onions, diced
2 cans (15 ounces each) tomato sauce
1 can (6 ounces) tomato paste
1 can (4 ounces) sliced mushrooms

1 tablespoon Worcestershire sauce
1 teaspoon basil leaves
1 teaspoon salt
¼ teaspoon pepper
⅛ teaspoon garlic powder
1 pound spaghetti

In a large skillet fry sausage until almost brown. Add green pepper and onion; cook until tender. Stir in tomato sauce, paste and mushrooms with liquid. (I just add 1 can of tomato puree and 1 can of drained mushrooms.) Add Worcestershire, basil, salt, pepper and garlic powder. Simmer uncovered 20 minutes. Prepare 1 pound spaghetti according to package directions. Drain. Arrange spaghetti on a large platter and pour on sauce. Serves 6-8.

## ROAST ROCK CORNISH GAME HEN
## WITH RICE STUFFING

### Penny L. Brant
### Huron County

2 Rock Cornish Hens (18-24 ounces)
2 teaspoons margarine
¼ cup margarine, melted
1¾ cups chicken stock
½ teaspoon salt
½ tablespoon margarine
½ cup long grain, brown rice
1 carrot, shredded
2 to 3 tablespoons chopped parsley
Cherry tomatoes, garnish

Clean hens thoroughly; place 1 teaspoon margarine in each cavity and place, breasts up, in a roaster pan. Season ¼ cup melted margarine to taste; baste hen breasts, and set aside.

Bring chicken stock to a boil in a medium size saucepan. Add salt, ½ tablespoon margarine, and rice; stir. Cover tightly and cook over low heat for 30 minutes.

When rice has cooked for 30 minutes, place hens in preheated 375°F. oven, for 20 minutes, while rice continues to cook. After 20 minutes, remove rice from heat, add shredded carrot and parsley; stir well. Remove slightly cooked hens from oven, and stuff with rice mixture.

Return hens to oven for 1 to 1½ hours. Garnish with cherry tomatoes and chopped parsley. Serves two.


## NO-CRUST PIZZA

### Jamie Stewart
### Madison County

1 can (8 ounces) pizza sauce
1 pound ground beef
1 small onion, chopped
½ cup packaged dry bread crumbs
½ teaspoon salt
¼ teaspoon oregano
2 pimiento-stuffed or pitted black olives
½ cup shredded mozzarella cheese
½ cup shredded cheddar cheese
4 slices canned pimiento

Measure out ½ cup pizza sauce; mix with ground beef, onion, bread crumbs, salt and oregano in a bowl. Divide the ground beef mixture into 4 or 5 equal patties. Place several inches apart on ungreased jelly roll pan. Pat each into a circle. Pinch the edge of each circle to make a stand-up rim. Pour about 2 tablespoons of the remaining pizza sauce into the center of each circle and spread it to the edge. Bake in preheated 425°F. oven 15 to 20 minutes. While pizzas are baking, cut 2 or 3 olives crosswise into slices (enough for eyes). Remove pizzas and turn off oven. Sprinkle each pizza with about 2 tablespoons mozzarella cheese for a face and 2 tablespoons cheddar cheese around the edge for hair. Use the olives for eyes and pimiento slices for the mouth. Return pizzas to warm oven and heat about 5 minutes or until cheese melts.

## FRANK 'n BEAN CASSEROLE

1 pound baked beans or pork and
   beans
½ medium onion, chopped fine (or 1½
   teaspoons instant minced onion)
¼ teaspoon salt
1 tablespoon prepared mustard
⅓ cup molasses or sorghum
⅓ cup chili sauce or ketchup

4 to 6 frankfurters, sliced
  OR: 3 to 4 slices luncheon meat

Preheat oven to 400°F. Mix all ingredients but the meat in a 1-quart baking dish. Arrange the frankfurters or luncheon meat on top. Bake about 30 minutes.

    To save time, mix all ingredients together in a heavy skillet or saucepan. Cook on top of the range until the flavors are blended, about 10 or 15 minutes. Makes 3 to 4 servings.

## RIO GRANDE PORK ROAST

### LeAnn Hemmings
### Adams County

4 to 5 pound pork roast
½ teaspoon salt

½ teaspoon garlic salt
½ teaspoon chili powder

Season roast with spices. Place fat side up in roaster pan. Insert meat thermometer in thickest part of meat. Roast at 325°F. until thermometer registers 170°F. or allow 30 to 40 minutes per pound. Brush on Rio Grande Glaze during last 20 to 30 minutes. Let stand 10 minutes before carving.

**RIO GRANDE GLAZE**
½ cup apple jelly
1 tablespoon vinegar

½ cup catsup
½ teaspoon chili powder

Combine all ingredients in a saucepan. Bring to boil, reduce heat, simmer 2 minutes.

## MACARONI AND CHEESE

### Beth Biery
### Hancock County

8 ounces elbow macaroni
¼ cup butter
¼ cup flour
1 teaspoon salt
⅛ teaspoon pepper

2 cups milk
1 cup chunked ham
8 ounces cheddar cheese, shredded
(2 cups)

Cook macaroni, drain. Melt butter in medium saucepan. Remove from heat. Stir in flour, salt, pepper. Gradually add milk. Stir in ham, cheese, and macaroni. Stir before serving.

## BROCCOLI RICE CASSEROLE

### Lisa Baldridge
### Richland County

1 2-pound package cheese spread
(Velveeta)
1 can cream of celery soup
1 can cream of mushroom soup

½ package onion soup mix
4 cups cooked rice
1 package (20 ounces) frozen broccoli

Dice cheese. Add remaining ingredients and mix well. Place in casserole. Bake uncovered at 325°F. for approximately 30 minutes.

## VEGETABLE SOUP WITH PORK

### Susanne Linnean
### Logan County

Pork back bone
2 quarts tomato juice
1 onion, minced
1 cup peas
1 cup corn

3 large potatoes, diced
2 carrots, sliced
1 pint green beans
1 cup shredded cabbage

Boil pork in tomato juice until tender. Add vegetables and simmer until tender.

## SAVORY SPAGHETTI WITH MEAT SAUCE

### Kristi Ann Armbruster
### Henry County

| | |
|---|---|
| 2 strips bacon, cut up | 1 teaspoon oregano |
| 1¼ pounds ground beef | ¼ teaspoon garlic powder |
| Salt and pepper to your taste | 1 tablespoon sugar |
| 2 tablespoons diced onion | 1 can (28 ounces) whole tomatoes |
| 1 tablespoon diced green pepper | 1 can (8 ounces) tomato sauce |
| ½ teaspoon sweet basil | 8 ounces uncooked spaghetti |

Lightly brown bacon; add ground beef and brown. Drain fat. Add salt and pepper, onion, green pepper, sweet basil, oregano, garlic powder, and sugar.

Blend can of whole tomatoes in blender. Add tomatoes and tomato sauce to meat. Bring to boil, then let simmer for ½ hour. While sauce is simmering, cook spaghetti for 8 minutes in water to which 1 tablespoon salt and 1 tablespoon oil has been added. Drain and add to meat sauce; let simmer for ½ hour to an hour.

NOTE: The recipe is a specialty of my aunt's.

## SWEET-SOUR CHICKEN KABOBS

### Tami Nicol
### Union County

**MARINADE**

| | |
|---|---|
| ½ cup soy sauce | ½ cup reserved pineapple juice |
| ¼ cup cooking oil | 1 teaspoon dry mustard |
| 1 tablespoon brown sugar | 2 teaspoons ground ginger |
| 1 teaspoon garlic salt | ¼ teaspoon freshly ground pepper |

**KABOBS**

| | |
|---|---|
| 2 whole chicken breasts, skinned and boned | 1 can water chestnuts (whole) |
| 1 can pineapple chunks, drained | 8 cherry tomatoes |
| 2 green peppers, cut in bite-size pieces | 8 large mushroom caps |

Combine marinade ingredients in a small saucepan; simmer 5 minutes. Cool. Cut chicken into bite-size pieces. Marinate pieces for one hour, stirring occasionally. Drain, reserving marinade. Thread chicken pieces, pineapple chunks, green pepper pieces, water chestnuts, cherry tomatoes, and mushroom caps on metal skewers. Grill or broil 20 minutes basting with reserved marinade.

### JAMBALAYA

**Susan Doliboa**
**Warren County**

**Jeanne Clouse**
**Mercer County**

2 tablespoons butter or margarine
½ cup diced onion
¼ cup diced green pepper
1 pound ground beef
1 can (1 pound 12 ounces) tomatoes

1 teaspoon salt
½ teaspoon sugar
¼ teaspoon thyme
1 small bay leaf
1⅓ cups precooked rice

Melt butter or margarine in skillet over medium heat. Add onion, green pepper and ground beef.

Cook, stirring often, until meat is browned. If a large amount of fat cooks out, spoon off excess.

Drain tomatoes, measuring juice. Add water to juice to make 1½ cups.

Add the liquid, tomatoes, salt, sugar, thyme, and bay leaf to mixture in the skillet.

Cover and simmer 5 minutes. Stir in rice, cover and simmer 5 minutes longer. Discard bay leaf before serving.

**Mary Sparks**
**Madison County**

Used the same recipe as above, but made one substitution: Instead of 1 pound ground beef, she used ½ cup diced cooked ham and 1 pound cleaned shrimp.

### PORK KABOBS

**Katie Snyder**
**Wyandot County**

2 pounds fresh pork butt
2 tablespoons chili sauce
2 tablespoons honey
1 teaspoon curry powder

¼ cup soy sauce
1 tablespoon salad oil
1 tablespoon minced green onion
3 medium onions, each cut into quarters

About 4½ hours before serving or early in the day, trim excess fat from pork butt; cut meat into 1 inch cubes. In bowl, combine chili sauce, honey, curry powder, soy sauce, oil and green onion. Stir in meat. Cover; refrigerate at least 3 hours, stirring occasionally.

About 1 hour before serving, on four 18-inch skewers, thread pork cubes alternately with onions, reserving marinade. Place skewers on grill; cook about 20 minutes or until pork is tender, basting frequently with marinade and turning occasionally. Makes 4 servings.

## MOUSSAKA

### Sarah DeWeese
### Shelby County

| | |
|---|---|
| 1 pound hamburger | ¼ cup butter |
| 2 cups chopped onions | ½ cup flour |
| ½ cup water | 3 cups milk |
| ¼ cup ketchup | ⅛ teaspoon salt |
| 1 tablespoon chopped parsley | ⅛ teaspoon nutmeg |
| 1 teaspoon salt | 2 egg yolks |
| ⅛ teaspoon pepper | 1 large eggplant (about 2 pounds) |
| 1 cup fine bread crumbs | ¼ cup fat |
| 2 slightly beaten egg whites | ¼ cup shredded cheese |

Brown hamburger in heavy skillet. Add onion, water, ketchup, parsley, 1 teaspoon salt and pepper. Simmer 10 minutes. Combine bread crumbs with egg whites; add half of mixture to meat mixture.

Make a white sauce from butter, flour and milk, ⅛ teaspoon salt, and nutmeg. Add a little of white sauce to egg yolks; return to saucepan. Cook until thick.

Pare eggplant and cut into ½-inch slices. Brown slices in hot fat. Place half of slices in bottom of a buttered baking dish (12 × 8 × 2-inches). Spread half the meat mixture over the eggplant.

Add 1 cup of white sauce. Add second layer of eggplant, meat and remaining white sauce. Mix cheese with remaining bread crumb mixture. Spread over top layer of white sauce. Bake in a 350°F. oven for 30 minutes.

## TACO SALAD

### Cathi Melcher
### Wood County

| | |
|---|---|
| 1 pound hamburger | 4 medium tomatoes, sliced |
| 1 package taco seasoning | 8 ounces cheddar cheese, coarsely grated |
| 1 medium head lettuce, torn | 1 package tortilla chips |
| 1 small can kidney beans | |
| 1 large onion, chopped | |

**DRESSING**

| | |
|---|---|
| 16 ounces Thousand Island dressing | 1 tablespoon taco seasoning |
| ⅔ cup sugar | 1 tablespoon taco sauce |

Brown hamburger; add taco seasoning, reserving 1 tablespoon seasoning for dressing.

In a large bowl, layer lettuce, meat mixture, kidney beans, onion, tomatoes and cheese.

Combine all ingredients for dressing. (Dressing is best made the day before.)

Add chips and dressing just before serving.

# PRESERVED FOODS

## STRAWBERRY JELLY

### Jean Starr
### Seneca County

3 quarts fresh strawberries
7½ cups granulated sugar

¼ cup lemon juice
2 pouches fruit pectin

Wash and remove caps from berries. Crush. Place in a dampened jelly bag and let drip to extract juice. Stir sugar and lemon juice into juice. Bring to a full boil, stirring constantly. Stir in fruit pectin all at once. Stir and bring to a full rolling boil; boil hard one minute. Remove from heat. Skim off foam. Immediately ladle into hot glasses or jars, leaving ½ inch space at top of glasses, ⅛ inch at top of jars. Wipe any spills from rims. Spoon ⅛ inch hot paraffin onto hot jelly surfaces. Prick any air bubbles. Let stand to cool. Store in a cool, dry place.

## PEACH MARMALADE

### Patty Beach
### Ashland County

4 cups peeled, mashed peaches
4 cups sugar

1 whole orange, put through meat grinder, rind and all

Combine ingredients in a saucepan. Cook slowly until thick. Put in containers and seal. Boil in hot water bath for 5 minutes.

## ONION CELERY SALT

### Becky Kreuz
### Fulton County

Chop onions and place on cookie sheets, spreading evenly. Use 1 to 2 pounds of chopped onion per cookie sheet. (The lighter load dries faster.) Place sheets in a 150°F. oven. About every ½ hour, stir or turn pieces so they will dry evenly. Reverse trays (upper to lower, etc.) every hour. Most vegetables take 4 to 12 hours to dry. When cooled, they should be very crisp.

Wash celery leaves and place on cookie sheets, spreading evenly. Dry as for onions, stirring frequently. These will dry MUCH faster.

For the onion/celery salt recipe, I used 5 cookie sheets of onions and 4 sheets of celery leaves. When dry, I blended ALL in an electric blender, and added 2 tablespoons of table salt. This makes about ⅔ cup of actual seasoned salt . . . so one can readily see why the commercial salts have a high price tag!

## CANNED TOMATOES

### Diane Mehbod
### Montgomery County

1. Check to be sure jars are perfect.
2. Wash jars, lids, and bands as directed.
3. Select the best tomatoes; enough for 1 canner load.
4. Wash tomatoes.
5. Cut up imperfect tomatoes. Cook just until soft. Puree in blender. Strain juice and reserve.
6. Scald good tomatoes, remove skin.
7. Put tomatoes in jars. Cover with juice. Add ½ teaspoon of salt, ¼ teaspoon citric acid for pints. Add 1 teaspoon of salt and ½ teaspoon citric acid to quarts.
8. Place jars in boiling water to 1½ inches of top.
9. Heat pints 7 minutes, quarts 10 minutes. Leave them uncovered to drive out air and gases.
10. Remove. Wipe. Seal jars. Return to boiling water.
11. Add boiling water to cover 1 to 2 inches above tops of jars.
12. Process 20 minutes for pints, 30 minutes for quarts.
13. Remove, let cool, test for seal. Store in a cool, dry place out of direct sunlight.

## CANNED GOLDEN BEETS

### Diana Leopard
### Union County

Pick beets at their prime harvesting time to ensure good taste and good quality. Clean beets of soil and cut tops to about 1 inch above beet. Boil beets in water for 10 to 15 minutes so the skins and tops will slip off easily. Remove skin and tops and cut beets in desired shapes. Place in water; bring to boil again and heat for about 5 minutes. Then fill hot canning jars with beets. Add ½ teaspoon salt to each pint jar. Fill jars with water in which the beets were cooked to ½ inch from top of jar. Put on lids and caps tightly. Put 2 quarts hot water in pressure canner. Place jars on rack inside canner and secure lid properly. Bring canner to a full steam and let steam escape through stem vent for 7 minutes. Then apply stop cock. Pressure inside canner should reach 10 pounds and not go over or below that. Adjust heat to maintain 10 pounds pressure. Process beets for 35 minutes for pint jars. When 35 minutes is up, turn off heat and let pressure go down to zero. Open steam vent and wait 3 minutes. Remove canner lid away from you and cover canner with a cloth for 3 minutes. Take out jars and place in a draft free place. After 12 to 24 hours, check jars for proper seal. Label jars before storing. Remember to follow the directions of your canner to be safe.

## FRUIT LAYER GATEAU

### Jody Boes
### Seneca County

**CAKE**

4 eggs, separated
3 tablespoons lukewarm water
⅔ cup sugar
Grated peel of ½ lemon

1 cup all-purpose flour
Scant ½ cup cornstarch
1 teaspoon baking powder

**FILLING**

4 ounces nougat
1 cup ground almonds
1½ tablespoons kirsch

3 tablespoons water
1 tablespoon powdered sugar, sifted

**TOPPING**

⅓ cup apricot jam
¾ cup toasted sliced almonds

1½ cups mixed fruit

**GLAZE**

¼ cup sugar
2¼ teaspoons cornstarch
Dash of salt

½ cup orange juice
1 teaspoon grated orange peel
1½ teaspoons orange flavored liqueur

Grease a 10-inch springform pan. Preheat oven to 375°F.

To make cake, put egg yolks, water, half the sugar and lemon peel into a large bowl. Beat until pale and creamy, 5 to 10 minutes, with an electric mixer. Beat egg whites until stiff; fold in remaining sugar. Fold egg white mixture into egg yolk mixture. Sift flour with cornstarch and baking powder. Fold into egg mixture. Turn batter into greased pan. Bake 40 minutes or until a wooden pick inserted in center comes out clean. Turn cake out onto a rack to cool. Cut cooled cake horizontally into three layers.

To make filling, melt nougat in a double boiler over low heat. Spread over one cake layer. Cover with second layer. Combine almonds, kirsch, water and powdered sugar in a small bowl. Spread over second layer. Cover with third cake layer.

To make Topping, warm jam and press through a strainer to obtain jelly. Brush warm jelly over top and sides of cake. Cover sides with sliced almonds, pressing in well. Prepare fresh fruit or drain canned fruit; arrange on top of cake.

To make Glaze, mix sugar, cornstarch and salt in a small saucepan. Gradually stir in orange juice until smooth. Heat to boiling, stirring constantly. Boil and stir 2 minutes. Add orange peel and orange flavored liqueur. Cover and cool. Spoon cooled glaze over fruit.

## KRANSEKAKE
## (GARLAND CAKE)

### Laura Bix
### Delaware County

1 pound almonds, ground (5⅓ cups)    3 egg whites
1 pound powdered sugar

**GLAZE**
  1 cup powdered sugar    3 drops vinegar
  1 egg white

Grind almonds in grinder; do not use a blender. Mix almonds and powdered sugar with your hands. Add egg whites; mix in with hands. Roll out dough to about the thickness of your little finger. Bake in greased kransekake pans at 300°F. for about 20 minutes. Let cool completely before removing from pan. Mix together ingredients for Glaze. Stack with largest cake on bottom, adding glaze before placing next cake on top.
    Note: My neighbors Tersa and Ole Jacobson lent me the pans and the recipe.


## 'CHOCOLATL' BROWNIES

### Karen Eitel
### Pickaway County

### Polly Waruszewski
### Greene County

1 stick butter or margarine
2 squares (2 ounces) baking chocolate
1 cup sugar
2 eggs
1 teaspoon vanilla

½ cup chopped nuts
¾ cup sifted enriched flour
½ teaspoon baking powder
½ teaspoon salt

Preheat oven to moderate (350°F.). Melt butter and chocolate in saucepan over very low heat on top of the range. Remove from the heat and add sugar. Add one unbeaten egg; mix well with a fork; then add other egg and mix until all of the egg is combined. Add vanilla and nuts. Sift together flour, baking powder and salt on a piece of waxed paper. Add to chocolate mixture and mix thoroughly. Pour into 8-inch square baking pan. Bake 25 to 30 minutes. Remove from oven and set on rack to cool slightly. Cut in squares while still warm. Remove from pan when completely cool.

## CANNOLI (SICILIAN PASTRY) SHELLS

**Sharon Heinrich**
**Auglaize County**

1½ cups all-purpose flour
2 tablespoons granulated sugar
½ teaspoon salt
1 egg, well beaten

2 tablespoons firm butter or margarine, cut into tiny pieces
¼ cup dry Sauterne wine

Place flour, sugar and salt in a sifter; sift into a bowl. Make a well in the center of the dry ingredients. Place egg and butter in well and stir with a fork from center to outside of well until flour mixture is moist. Add wine bit by bit (approximately a tablespoon at a time) until dough begins to cling together. Use as little wine as possible. Shape dough into ball, then knead until smooth (approximately five minutes). Cover and let rest fifteen minutes.

Roll dough out on floured board until paper thin, approximately ¹⁄₁₆ inch. (Dough will resist this, so keep working and be patient. Your dough should be elastic.) Cut into 3½-inch circles and gently roll into ovals with rolling pin. Wrap each oval around cannoli tube, placing the tube lengthwise on the oval. Seal edges with egg whites. Fry for approximately 1 minute until light golden brown in deep saucepan or fryer; oil should be about 2 inches deep and should completely cover shells. Use medium to high heat (350°). Remove cannoli tubes and shells with tongs and let drain 5 seconds on paper towel. Then slip out tube, handling shell carefully because it's very fragile. If you wait too long to remove shell from tube, it will be quite difficult. Cool shells completely. Fill immediately or store in air-tight container. Best when used within three days.

Makes approximately 25.

## CANNOLI FILLING

**Sharon Heinrich**
**Auglaize County**

**RICOTTA FILLING**
2 pounds (4 cups) ricotta cheese

Whirl in blender until very smooth or press through wire strainer.

Beat in:
1½ cups powdered sugar

4 teaspoons vanilla extract

When thoroughly mixed add:
½ cup finely chopped candied citron
¼ cup chopped milk chocolate

½ cup finely chopped candied orange peel

Stir to spread through filling. Cover and chill several hours or as long as three days.

*continued*

## CANNOLI FILLING (continued)

### STRAWBERRY (OR FRUIT) FILLING

 1 carton (24 ounces) ricotta cheese          1 package (8 ounces) cream cheese

Whirl until smooth in blender.

1¼ cup powdered sugar          1 tablespoon vanilla extract

Add gradually until thoroughly mixed. Refrigerate until almost ready to serve.

1½ cup drained frozen (or fresh) strawberries or other fruit

Gently mix into cheese. Serve immediately or berries may juice.

### FLUFFY FILLING

Prepare only half of either Plain Ricotta or Fruit Filling and refrigerate. Just before serving whip until stiff:

 1 cup heavy whipping cream

Gently fold into mixture.

### QUICK FILLING

Prepare any flavor of pudding according to directions. Chill

### PISTACHIO FILLING

To any of the preceding fillings, add a few drops of green food coloring to tint pale green. Garnish with chopped blanched pistachios.

Note: Although both shells and filling may be made ahead, put together just before serving to retain fresh, crisp shells.

*To Make Cannoli Tubes:*

Use commercial tubes or make your own. Purchase 1 inch diameter lightweight aluminum (preferred) or chrome tubing at a hardware store. Cut it to 4½-inch or 5-inch lengths. Be sure all edges are smooth.

*To Fill Cannoli Shells:*

You may use a plain large pastry tube to force filling into shells. As a substitute, put filling into plastic bag and cut a very tiny hole in the corner. Or use a small spoon to fill shells. Fill only the number of shells you plan to serve at once.

*To Garnish:*

Sift powdered sugar. Decorate ends with sweet chocolate shavings, candied cherries, strawberries, or other fruit on top.

Serve on doilies for buffet to aid serving and add delicate touch.

## DAZZLING DESSERT—FRUIT AND CREAM TART

### Karen Weck
### Van Wert County

Pastry for two 9-inch pie crusts
1 package (3 ounces) cream cheese
¾ cup sugar
1 tablespoon milk
1 teaspoon orange flavoring
⅔ cup heavy cream
2 tablespoons cornstarch
¼ cup water
½ cup orange juice
¼ cup lemon juice
1 pint strawberries
2 medium bananas, sliced
1 can (11 ounces) mandarin orange segments, drained

Roll out pastry to 15-inch circle. Place in 14-inch pizza pan. Form ½ inch rim; flute edges. Prick crust with fork. Bake at 350°F. for 12 minutes or until golden brown. Cool on rack.

Combine cream cheese, ¼ cup of the sugar, milk and orange flavoring. Beat until smooth. Add heavy cream; beat until thick. Spread over crust and chill.

Combine ½ cup sugar and cornstarch in saucepan. Stir in water, orange juice, and lemon juice. Cook, stirring until mixture boils. Cook one minute.

Reserve 3 strawberries. Hull and slice remaining berries, and arrange around inner edge of crust. Then add a ring of bananas, a ring of mandarin oranges and a ring of bananas. Spoon on sauce over fruit. Place whole berries in center. Chill two hours, or overnight to allow flavors to blend.

Note: This looks a lot prettier if the larger berries are used. Also it might take a quart of berries to pick from. Uniform size means a lot. Bananas are in a layered form.

## OATMEAL DROP COOKIES

### Melissa Thomas
### Washington County

1 cup enriched flour
½ teaspoon soda
½ teaspoon salt
½ cup butter or margarine, softened
¼ cup sugar
½ cup brown sugar
1 egg, unbeaten
1 teaspoon vanilla
2 tablespoons milk
2 cups rolled oats (quick cooking or regular)
½ cup raisins, chopped dates or nuts, if desired

Preheat oven to moderate 375°F. Sift flour and measure. Sift flour with soda and salt into mixing bowl. Add butter or margarine, sugar, brown sugar, egg, vanilla and milk. Mix until smooth.

Add rolled oats, and raisins, dates or nuts, if used. Stir until mixed.

Drop by spoonfuls about 2 inches apart on ungreased cookie sheets. Use one teaspoon to dip out the dough and the other to push onto the cookie sheet.

Bake for 10 to 12 minutes. The cookies will be a light golden color when they are done.

Remove cookies from pan with a spatula. Place on racks or paper toweling to cool.

# APPLE CRISP

**Loretta Faldowski**
**Jefferson County**

1 cup rolled oats (quick cooking or regular)
½ cup sifted, enriched flour
½ cup brown sugar, firmly packed
¼ teaspoon salt

**Kevin Sendelbach**
**Seneca County**

1 teaspoon cinnamon
½ cup butter or margarine, softened
4 cups peeled, sliced tart apples

Preheat oven to moderate (350°F.). Place rolled oats, flour, sugar, salt, and cinnamon in the bowl and mix to blend. Add butter or margarine and blend well with pastry blender or fork. Arrange peeled, sliced apples in buttered baking dish. Spread oatmeal mixture on top of apples and press down lightly. Bake about 30 minutes or until topping is brown and apples are tender when tested with a fork. Serve warm or cold with milk, cream, or ice cream.

Variations: In place of the fresh apples, use 4 cups sliced, fresh apricots, or peeled, sliced, fresh peaches or cut rhubarb, or 3 cups canned apple slices drained.

# EASTER NEST COFFEE CAKE

**Peggy Strow**
**Wood County**

1 package active dry yeast
½ cup milk
¼ cup sugar
¼ cup shortening

1 teaspoon salt
3 cups flour
1 egg, slightly beaten

Shredded coconut
Green food coloring

Confectioner's icing
Candy decorations

Soften yeast in ¼ cup warm water (110°F.). Heat milk, sugar, shortening, and salt till sugar dissolves; cool to lukewarm. Stir in 1 cup of flour; beat until smooth. Add softened yeast and egg; beat well. Stir in enough remaining flour to make a soft dough. Knead on lightly floured surface until smooth and elastic (8 to 10 minutes). Place in greased bowl; turn once. Cover; let rise in warm place until double (about one hour). Punch dough down; divide into thirds. Cover; let rest 10 minutes.

Shape ⅓ of dough into six "eggs;" place close together in center of greased baking sheet. For "nest," shape remaining dough into two 26-inch ropes; twist together. Coil around "eggs;" seal ends. Cover; let rise in warm place till double (approximately one hour). Bake at 375°F. for 15-20 minutes. Remove from sheet; cool.

Tint coconut with a few drops of green food coloring. Frost coffee cake with confectioner's icing. Sprinkle "eggs" with candy decorations and "nest" with tinted coconut.

**Confectioner's Icing:**
Combine 1 cup sifted powdered sugar, ¼ teaspoon vanilla, and enough milk to make a drizzling consistency (about 1½ tablespoons).

## FANCY PUDDING

### Kim Wood
### Montgomery County

1 (6-ounce) box vanilla pudding
3 cups milk
Sliced bananas

Orange juice
Chocolate cookies, crushed

Combine pudding mix and milk. Stir over medium heat until mixture comes to a boil. Refrigerate. Fill glasses half full with pudding. Then layer banana slices dipped in orange juice. Fill the rest of the way with pudding and sprinkle with chocolate cookie crumbs.

## BUTTERSCOTCH-WALNUT LOAF

### Liette Gidlow
### Licking County

1 package active dry yeast
¼ cup warm water (110°F.)
¼ cup milk (scalded and cooled)
¼ cup sugar

½ teaspoon salt
1 egg
¼ cup shortening
2¼ cups flour

FILLING
2 tablespoons butter, at room temperature
¼ cup sugar

3 teaspoons cinnamon

TOPPING
½ cup butter
½ cup packed brown sugar

½ cup chopped walnuts

Dissolve yeast in warm water in large mixing bowl. Stir in milk, sugar, salt, egg, shortening and 1¼ cups of the flour. Beat until smooth. Stir in enough remaining flour to make dough easy to handle.

Turn dough onto lightly floured surface; knead until smooth and elastic, about 5 minutes. Place in greased bowl; turn greased side up. Cover; let rise in warm place until double, about 1½ hours.

Punch down dough. Roll into a rectangle which has a width that is a multiple of 4 inches. Spread dough with the 2 tablespoons butter, and sprinkle with sugar and cinnamon. Cut into strips 4 inches wide. Stack strips vertically. Cut into strips 2 inches wide. Place small strips, cut side up, in loaf pan. Let rise until doubled about 45 minutes. Spread ½ cup butter and ½ cup brown sugar on top of loaf and bake in preheated 375°F. oven for 50 minutes. Sprinkle nuts on top of loaf halfway through baking time. Makes one large loaf.

A word to the wise—to prevent the butterscotch topping from boiling over onto your oven, either line the bottom oven rack with aluminum foil or bake the loaf in a pan large enough that the bread does not rise to the top edge of the pan after the second rising.

## SWEDISH TEA RING

### Theresa Miller
### Holmes County

½ cup melted butter
⅔ cup sugar
1 teaspoon salt
2¼ cups hot milk
1 package dry yeast

¼ cup warm water
1 egg, well beaten
1 teaspoon almond extract
7 cups of white flour

**TOPPING**
Melted butter
Sugar

Cinnamon
1½ cups raisins or candied fruit
1 cup almonds or walnuts, chopped

Mix the butter, sugar, salt and hot milk in a large bowl and let cool to lukewarm. Stir the yeast into ¼ cup warm water and let stand for five minutes to dissolve. Add the dissolved yeast, egg, almond extract and three cups of the flour to the first mixture and mix vigorously. Add three more cups of the flour and mix well. Turn out onto a lightly floured board, knead for a minute or two, and let rest for 10 minutes. Add the remaining flour only if the dough is too sticky; resume kneading until smooth and elastic. Put the dough in a large, buttered bowl, cover, and let rise in a warm place until double in bulk. Punch down, knead it for a minute or two, and divide it in half. Roll and shape the first piece with your hands into a long, thin roll. Using a rolling pin and an unfloured board, roll it into a thin rectangle about 7- by 16-inches; it will stick to the board but may easily be lifted with a knife. Spread with melted butter and sprinkle with sugar, cinnamon, ¾ cup raisins and ½ cup chopped walnuts. Starting with the long side, roll like a jelly roll. Trim if necessary and join the ends to form a ring. Place on a buttered cookie sheet; make perpendicular cuts with scissors about one inch apart and then spread open, so that one side falls flat. Repeat with the other piece of dough if you wish or use remaining dough for one loaf of Swedish Bread. Cover, let rise until double in bulk. Bake at 375°F. for 25 to 30 minutes.

## FRUIT 'N YOGURT DAZZLER

### Cynthia Laukhuf
### Paulding County

3 egg yolks
⅓ cup honey
¼ cup water
1 teaspoon cornstarch
2 cartons (8 ounces) plain yogurt

8 to 10 cups fresh fruits: strawberries, kiwi, peaches, honeydew, cantaloupe, grapes, plums, bananas
Toasted coconut

In a small saucepan combine egg yolks, honey, water, and cornstarch; mix well. Cook and stir over medium heat until mixture comes to a boil. Reduce heat; cook and stir 2 minutes longer. Spoon mixture into a small bowl or glass measuring cup. Cover with plastic wrap; chill, without stirring, several hours. At serving time, fold egg yolk mixture into yogurt, blending well. In a large glass bowl or individual parfait glasses, layer fruit and yogurt mixture, ending with yogurt on top. Sprinkle with toasted coconut and, if desired, garnish with fresh mint leaves. This makes quite a lot. I usually cut the recipe in half.

## SUNBURST COFFEE CAKE

**Tonya Willeke**
**Union County**

2½-3 cups all purpose flour
1 package active dry yeast
⅔ cup milk
¼ cup sugar
¼ cup shortening
1 teaspoon salt
1 egg
1 teaspoon finely shredded lemon peel

¼ cup raspberry, currant, cherry or strawberry jelly
1½ cups sifted powdered sugar
3 tablespoons lemon juice
¼ teaspoon vanilla
¼ cup chopped pecans or toasted sliced almonds

In large mixer bowl combine one cup of the flour and the yeast. In saucepan heat milk, sugar, shortening, and salt just until warm (115° to 120°F.) and shortening is almost melted; stir constantly. Add to the flour mixture; stir in egg and lemon peel. Beat at low speed on electric mixer for ½ minute, scraping sides of bowl constantly. Beat 3 minutes at high speed. Stir in as much of the remaining flour as you can mix in with a spoon.

Turn out onto lightly floured surface. Knead in enough of the remaining flour to make a moderately soft dough that is smooth and elastic (3 to 5 minutes total). Shape into a ball. Place in lightly greased bowl; turn once to grease surface. Cover; let rise in warm place until double (1 to 1½ hours).

Punch down. Cover; let rest 10 minutes. Roll out into a 10 × 8-inch rectangle. With floured doughnut cutter, cut into 12 doughnuts; arrange in a circle on greased baking sheet. Stretch the doughnut rings slightly with fingers to elongate. Cluster "holes" in center, cutting additional "holes" from dough scraps. Let rise until light (about 45 minutes). Bake in 375°F. oven for 12 to 15 minutes or until golden. Carefully remove from baking sheet. Cool on rack. Spoon choice of jelly into center of doughnut rings. Combine powdered sugar, lemon juice, and vanilla; drizzle over coffee cake. Sprinkle center with chopped pecans or toasted almonds.

Makes one coffee cake.

## APPLE CRISP

**Michele McGinnis**
**Pickaway County**

4 cups (approximately) diced apples
½ cup water
1 teaspoon cinnamon
1 tablespoon of lemon juice

⅓ cup butter
1 cup sugar
⅓ cup flour
1 cup rolled oats

Grease baking dish; put in apples, water, and cinnamon, and sprinkle with lemon juice. Mix butter, sugar, flour, and oats until crumbly; spread over apple mixture.

Bake uncovered in a moderate oven 350°F. for 30 to 45 minutes or until top is crispy golden brown. Serve warm or cold. Cream or ice cream can be used.

## WHOLE WHEAT COFFEE CAKE

### Lois Knoll
### Huron County

**REFRIGERATOR ROLL DOUGH**

2 packages yeast
2 cups warm water
½ cup sugar
1 teaspoon salt

2 cups wheat flour
2 eggs
5 tablespoons oil
4 cups white flour (approximately)

**TOPPING**

½ cup cream
½ cup brown sugar

Cinnamon

Dissolve yeast in warm water. Add sugar and salt. Stir. Add wheat flour; beat until smooth. Add eggs and oil. Beat. Add white flour. Turn out on lightly floured board and knead for 10 minutes. Refrigerate overnight. Will stay good in refrigerator for up to three days. Makes four coffee cakes or three dozen rolls.

Divide dough into four equal parts. Take one part and spread out in a 9-inch greased pan. Let rise. Punch small holes in the dough with finger tip. Pour ½ cup cream on the dough and in the holes. Sprinkle on ½ cup brown sugar and top with a few sprinkles of cinnamon. Bake at 400°F. for 15 to 20 minutes. Serves 8.

Note: The roll dough recipe is my recipe and the topping for the cake is my mother's, June Knoll.

## SWEDISH COFFEE RING

### Diana Alspaugh
### Warren County

1 tablespoon yeast
¼ cup warm water
¼ cup shortening
¾ cup milk, scalded
¼ cup sugar

1 egg
¼ teaspoon salt
½ teaspoon cardamom (ground)
3 to 4 cups white flour

**FILLING**

¼ cup butter
¼ cup brown sugar

½ cup almond paste

Dissolve yeast in water and let stand until bubbly. Meanwhile heat shortening and milk together; when cool, add to yeast and water. Stir in sugar, egg, salt, cardamom and flour; mix until dough pulls away from sides of bowl. Knead dough on floured board. When dough becomes smooth and is not sticky, place in greased bowl and turn dough over to grease the top. Cover and let rise 45 minutes. While dough is rising, mix ingredients for filling together (it should be spreadable). Punch down dough and roll into a rectangle on lightly floured board. Spread with filling and roll up. On a greased cookie sheet, bring ends together and join. With clean scissors cut ¾ of the way into the dough, and cut evenly around the ring. Turn pieces so filling is facing upwards. Let rise 45 minutes. Bake at 350°F. for 15 to 20 minutes. Decorate with almonds, candied fruit or icing or with all three.

## SAVARIN
### Joan Grimes
### Brown County

**SAVARIN DOUGH**

3 tablespoons sugar
1 cup warm milk (110°F.)
1½ packages active dry yeast
3 cups all purpose flour
½ cup and 2 tablespoons butter or margarine

4 eggs
1 tablespoon vanilla
½ teaspoon salt
¼ cup raisins, optional

**SAVARIN SYRUP**

1 cup sugar
1 cup boiling water

¼ cup orange liqueur

**SAVARIN GLAZE**

½ cup apricot preserves

2 tablespoons sugar

Stir 1 teaspoon of the sugar into warm milk and sprinkle with yeast. Let stand 5 minutes or until the surface is frothy. Stir gently to moisten any dry particles remaining on top. Sift flour into a large bowl. Melt butter; cool slightly. Beat eggs with remaining sugar in a medium bowl until frothy; add vanilla, salt, and melted butter. Stir egg mixture into yeast mixture. Pour into flour, mixing well to almost pouring consistency. Cover and let rise in a warm place for 10 minutes.

Grease and flour a 9-inch savarin pan. Add raisins to mixture and pour into prepared pan. Cover and let rise till dough has risen almost to top of pan. Bake in a 425°F. oven for 40 minutes or until golden brown. Turn out on a wire rack. Cool.

**Savarin Syrup and Glaze:**

Heat one cup sugar and one cup water to boiling; reduce heat. Simmer uncovered two minutes; cool to lukewarm. Stir in liqueur. Slowly drizzle syrup on Savarin until all syrup is absorbed.

Press apricot preserves through strainer. Heat preserves and sugar to boiling, stirring constantly; reduce heat. Simmer one or two minutes until slightly thickened. Cool 10 minutes. Spread glaze over Savarin.

Savarin can be served with fresh fruit and whipped cream.

## AUNT ORPHA'S CHERRY COBBLER
### Molly Hutchinson
### Williams County

1 cup sugar
1 cup milk
2 teaspoons baking powder
Pinch of salt

1¾ cup flour
1 cup cherries

Mix all ingredients together and put in greased 9 × 13 × 2-inch pan. Cover with additional 1½ cups cherries, 1 cup sugar, small lump of butter, and 2 cups boiling water. Bake uncovered at 350°F. for one hour.

Note: This is an old family recipe. Aunt Orpha was my great-great aunt on my father's side of the family.

## 4-H TODAY

4-H is the youth education program of the Cooperative Extension Service, which is conducted jointly by the U.S. Department of Agriculture, The Ohio State University, and county government.

The Extension Service was established to educate and to interpret research. Today, the Extension Service and its 4-H programs serve people in towns, cities and rural areas with information on agriculture, home economics, community development and related subjects.

Volunteer advisors are the backbone of the 4-H program. Agents provide training for advisors and they, in turn, teach youth groups.

The 4-H program is for all young people between nine (or in the 3rd grade) and 19, from all racial, cultural, economic and social backgrounds.

## LEARN BY DOING

Four-H is a "learn by doing" educational program with many and varied projects and activities. Included are life long skills in leadership, citizenship and decision making, to help boys and girls achieve their fullest potential.

Four-H has a place for you—as a member, leader, parent, or sponsor.

## THE OHIO 4-H FOUNDATION

The Ohio 4-H Foundation is proud to cooperate with counties throughout Ohio in making this Ohio 4-H Blue Ribbon Cookbook possible.

The Ohio 4-H Foundation is the official organization for soliciting and receiving gifts for 4-H in Ohio.

For information about the 4-H Foundation or other activities, call or write:

State 4-H Office
2120 Fyffe Road
Columbus, Ohio 43210
(614) 422-5936